IN SEARCH OF JUSTICE

FROM TRAGEDY TO HOPE

IDA MARIE KREISER

In Search of Justice

From Tragedy To Hope

Ida Marie Kreiser, Author

PipStones, LLC.
P.O. Box 4507
Fort Walton Beach, FL. 32549
www.pipstones.com
aturner@pipstones.com

Copyright ©2023 by PipStones Publishing (PipStones, LLC.)
All rights reserved. This book or any portion thereof may not be reproduced or used in any manner whatsoever without the written permission of the author except for the use of brief quotation in a book review.

Unless otherwise noted, all scripture is taken from the New King James Version®. Copyright ©1982 by Thomas Nelson. Used by permission. All rights reserved.

Editor, Abigail Turner
Assistant Editor, Deborah Hoffman
Designed by PipStones, LLC.
Foreword By Margaret McLemore

Library of Congress Control Number: 2023943250
ISBN-13: 978-1-7328594-9-4, Paperback
ISBN-13: 978-1-7328594-0-1, E-book
For Worldwide Distribution. Printed in the United States of America.

DRIVE
SAFELY
IN MEMORY
Joshua M Kreiser

Table of Contents

Dedication

This book is dedicated to all victims of hit-and-run, cyberstalking attacks, and various types of murder.

I wrote this in honor of my son, Joshua, and my friends who have stood beside me through tough times.

Some friends are still alive, and some have passed on into heaven.

Foreword

While I was Mayor of my small town, I received a call one day from a woman named Ida, wanting the city to pass a Proclamation concerning hit-and-run accidents.

We talked several times over the phone and drafted Proclamations. When it was time for the city to vote on the Proclamation, I met Ida Kreiser for the first time. What a joy and delight it has been getting to know Ida.

She is a loving, caring, grieving Christian woman trying to make her son's death in the hit-and-run have meaning. She has accomplished so much. Not only does she have a Proclamation in my city, but she has also had Proclamations passed in all the cities in our county.

Ida also had a streetlight installed where her son's accident took place. The State of Florida has agreed to pay for the streetlight. We are celebrating that today.

This book is a must-read for anyone grieving or if you know someone in the grieving process. Reading this book will touch your heart and soul. You will smile, laugh, and cry as you relate to Ida's story of her triumphs and tragedies. I wish I had this book many years ago when my sister was murdered.

I am reminded of Ecclesiastes 3:4. There is a season for all things. It is my sincere hope that this book will help other families dealing with the tragic loss of a loved one from any circumstance, including hit-and-run accidents.

Margaret Fishel McLemore
Former Mayor of Mary Esther, FL.

Introduction

The healing process from major tragedies can be complex. My story is full of mishaps, unforeseen circumstances, hateful and leud persons, and the death of two of the most important people in my life. From these things, hurt, anger, shock, and even denial worked their way into my mindset. The effect caused me to realize that I needed healing, resolution, and closure— I needed God's help.

Actions are often generationally influenced, but sometimes others cause us to make choices. I have made decisions to protect the people in my life, which I felt were correct at the time. We all have options, something that God instills in us from the beginning, and how we deal with these helps us move through life. My intentions were always good; if anyone was hurt, it was me. My involvement in assisting others may have caused a bit of a pebbled road.

God's perfect plan for every person is often riddled with distractions wrought by the Devil and made manifest through authority figures and our inclination to sin. Forgiving ourselves and others is a significant step in our relationship with God, our healer. I am working towards complete forgiveness and total peace.

I am finalizing this peace by writing this book and sharing my experiences. In that process, it is essential to forewarn you of the potential of bad happenings and how I dealt with them. Please be encouraged and know that no matter how awful things may look, there are people with similar stories. Some have conquered the giant, like how David slayed Goliath, yet some may still be trying to find suitable stones.

Justice in the natural, now that is a hurdle I may never understand. The system does not always work as it should. Money, power, politics, and time play a significant role in upholding justice. This is where the division is between peace and chaos. These things are only more stones to grasp, and I am learning how to sling them. I have continued to do my due diligence in helping improve the system and providing others with resources and avenues for dealing with similar tragic circumstances.

I hope you will find solace and peace through this book and a strengthening of your relationship with God.

"For with God nothing shall be impossible. And Mary said, Behold the handmaid of the Lord; be it unto me according to thy word."

Luke 1:37-38

*Please note that the names in the book may have an *asterisk in front of their name. This indicates a fictitious name to hide the true identities of the people in the book.*

1

What is Murder?

"The thief cometh not, but for to steal, and to kill, and to destroy: I am come that they may have life, and that they might have it more abundantly."

John 10:10

Sin is all around us. Murder is the manifestation of evil. The Bible talks about murder and the different types which are paralleled in today's times. Whether we reverted to Exodus when Moses was saved from murder or fast forward into the history of 1875 when Asa Magoon was hanged in Vermont because of lies about him, lives were changed and often terminated. Think about when the Jews were killed during the Holocaust, one of the worst times in history spurred on by evil. Today, we endure the horror of people being bombed or shot in what we think of as safe zones, schools, and fun places such as movie theaters. Another form of murder is using technology to destroy a person's identity. I feel my life has been defamed by lies, injustice, and intimidation from this type of source, the web. I may not have been buried in the ground, or my ashes poured into an urn, but people worked very hard to try and assassinate my existence.

There have been many tragic circumstances in my life, which I'll highlight in this book. I have fared well enough to stay alive, seek out many avenues to heal, and strive for arrival in truth. Justice, now that's the problematic factor. Will justice prevail in the natural? Will there be a sense of resolution to these travesties? How much can one person take without closure? The Bible says, "A man's spirit will endure sickness, but a crushed spirit who can bear?" (Proverbs 18:14).

December 30, 2020, was undoubtedly a horrifying nightmare I have been unable to wake from. My son, Joshua Kreiser, was killed at eight o'clock that evening by a hit-and-run driver in Mary Esther, Florida, along the roadside of Highway 98. Joshua was heading across the street on foot when a driver crashed into the side of him. The car sped off and was found ditched in a parking lot a short distance from the scene. The Highway Patrol did their job that night and found the car. For that, I am thankful.

Then, the dreaded knock on the door. It was as though my life was blown from my being. I immediately tried calling Joshua but there was no answer. My baby was gone. Other than the initial shock, screaming and crying were all I could express on that horrifying night.

There were many things that the authorities could have pursued for an arrest, and yet, they didn't. They had the car, its plates, evidence of Joshua's blood on the outside of it, and even DNA samples of the people in the vehicle. The car belonged to the mother of one of the people in the vehicle, so she reported it stolen instead of turning her son in (as the driver or the accomplice). For some reason, no one proceeded with an investigation or an arrest. Had someone come forward or not left the crime scene, you could call it an accident. That was no accident. Things were hidden and blanketed. Because of them fleeing the scene, this was considered as murder.

To this day, no one has appeared with information or a confession. The State of Florida Attorney's Office has deemed this a closed case. How's that for justice? Not only is the death of a child one thing that a mother should never have to face, but the absence of truth can damage the mindset. The wondering of who and questioning why creates little cracks in your heart; without healing, the divots grow.

The nightmare certainly didn't stop *or* start on that evening. Many other events created a chasm requiring vigilance, determination, guidance, and more healing. After the devastation of Joshua's death, while I was trying to make funeral arrangements, one of Josh's ex-girlfriends spread lies about me on Facebook. She even had her friends message me some horrible things. At that time, all this added to the devastation of Joshua's death and bore a hole into my spirit. I know I may never get justice in this life, but God will someday vindicate these issues.

I never really had a great relationship with either of Joshua's girlfriends (the mothers of Joshua's children), but I couldn't understand why one of them would be so cruel after Joshua died? So, you can only imagine the difficulties that I faced in being able to see either of my grandchildren. One grandaughter is nineteen now and the other is fourteen and still no relationship.

As for now, questions race into my thoughts and fill my head, but I believe God is in control, that the things God has helped me do because of the death of Joshua and other tragedies have saved human lives and, at the very least, made people aware.

My story is a journey toward healing.

Billboard On Highway 98
Okaloosa County, FL

2

Monster Man

"But in all things approving ourselves as the ministers of God, in much patience, in afflictions, in necessities, in distresses... by pureness, by knowledge, by longsuffering, by kindness, by the Holy Ghost, by love unfeigned..."

2 Corinthians 6:4

Many people have lied, deceived, and betrayed me. I can no longer hide the truth, so I'll start where the problems began. Years ago, a man named *Marty invaded my life. He paid people to lie about me and broke into my house, and threatened my family and friends. This man accused me of killing his father (Mr. Russell), whom I was a caretaker for after he became ill. He was like family to me, and I cared for him deeply.

Before Marty assassinated my existence, I had a decent life and a job and volunteered for my community. I had a healthy church environment, many friends, and participated in Relay for Life fundraisers. Now, friends who have known me for years have looked at the trash spewed about me by Marty and believed it because it looked so legit. He was an A-grade monster man with the internet at his fingertips. Whether it was physical stalking, cyberstalking, cyberbullying, or other electronic communication to frighten and harass someone, he did it to me. He tried to take my life from me!

This predator, Marty, created websites on the internet in my name with a dot com after it to torment me. My name, pictures, social security number, and lies were splashed all over the internet. He was calling me with spoofed phone calls. Later on, this caused other people to message me and say things like, "Your brother sexually abused your son." The crazy thing is, I don't even have a brother! Marty even sold my pictures on eBay with the word "Murderer" at the top and other photoshopped images of me and my family. How could he do this to someone?

The influence of Marty's actions even caused people to threaten me. They said they would steal my son's ashes if I didn't pay them. They were so delusional and deceived about what was happening that they didn't even know my son was buried. These were people whom were close to Joshua. As a mother, I had to ask myself, "Are they going to go to the cemetery to dig up my child?" What an awful feeling. Even my son's body was not safe? I felt like my life was going in a circle, with no end to the craziness.

Someone can put my name into Google, and that's all she wrote. I couldn't walk into a church or a grief meeting or see a neighbor without them hating me instantly for believing the lies on the web. Before this happened, I was part of society. Now, I am just an outcast because of all of this. The saddest part is when false accusations are spread on the internet, they can appear genuine. People would rather believe lies and gossip than the truth. If this could happen to me, it could happen to you, although I pray it doesn't.

Through all this, I discovered that Monster Man was very good at this sort of thing. I'm not so sure that he hasn't done this to others. He was very calculated and determined in his methods of sabotage. Marty may have preyed upon others in the past.
One of the many reasons for this book is to help those who have thought about suicide and want to give up. Light always shines on the path; sometimes, we must wait to see it. In the case of Monster Man, he did quit. I had to take legal action and a whole pile of junk to filter through, but God was victorious. All of that has stopped. Perhaps he's

moved on to another victim with his vengeful nature.
Follow through and be vigilant with the things stuck in your path. I have added scripture to remind you that you are not alone, and God will have the last say. Allow Him to guide you and comfort you even amid the darkness.

If it had not been for my son's love, the hope of uniting my own family, and, ultimately, the grace of God, I would have committed suicide. It was quite a rough time in my life.

"Fear thou not; for I am with thee: be not dismayed; for I am thy God: I will strengthen thee; I will help thee; yea, I will uphold thee with the right hand of my righteousness."

Isaiah 41:10

3

Pulling A Jonah

"But in all things approving ourselves as the ministers of God, in much patience, in afflictions, in necessities, in distresses... by pureness, by knowledge, by longsuffering, by kindness, by the Holy Ghost, by love unfeigned..."

2 Corinthians 6:4

While volunteering at my high school office, I read my personal file. I found out I was adopted. Memories of comments made, demeaning words, and the necessity of isolating and restrictive discipline throughout my life, flooded my mind. Of course, it all made sense! Daddy had been afraid the truth would come out and it did! My whole life was a lie and I had suffered for it.

Well, there I was; the big secret was out. "Daddy" wasn't my birth father. I had many questions and feelings that were flitting through my mind. I loved my dad. He was the one who raised me. I loved my mom. I asked myself how to deal with this, and I didn't know how because I was so young.

Please understand me, my parents were great; we had beautiful and not-so-great times, just like any other family. Much has to do with our perspective and projection on life, baggage, and generational curses passed down through our family.

At seventeen., I called a church camp friend in New Hampshire. I had left home and was traveling with only a brown bag of clothes. She never answered, so I walked until I finally entered a local pizza place and played pinball. I wanted to control my own life. I didn't much care at that point; I felt my life and world were utterly wrecked, but I was basically numb and full of fear.

Fear is a scary word. Jonah, from the Bible, feared God. God told him to go to the city of Nineveh to tell the people to stop their wicked ways and to live for God. Jonah refused out of fear until later. I can relate to Jonah on so many levels. Maybe you can, too.

I found out in 2000 that my mom feared thunderstorms, even though growing up, she protected me and never showed that in front of me. She would say thunder was the angels bowling, and lightning was them making a strike. What a great analogy, especially from someone afraid of thunderstorms.

I was fearful of being alone, but I was also stubborn. When my friend from church camp didn't answer my call, I definitely wasn't going to call my parents because I knew (or thought I knew with my seventeen-year-old brain) what my dad would say. He always said, "You make your bed; you lie in it." I was unsure what that meant, but said it often to many people, so it must have been significant. Because of this, I wouldn't cave in and call them.

I sat in that pizza place for a very long time, trying to decide what to do. Then, this boy and his friends walked in. I got up, ordered a Coke, and asked for change for a few dollars. I played another pinball game, and then he walked over to me, my future husband, Joshua's biological father. We talked a little about pinball, and I "wiped his bottom" on some of the games. Then we played some pool and sat down and talked some more.

I had nowhere to go; a hotel wouldn't let a seventeen-year-old check in, so he took me to his great-grandmother's old house, which was very small and barely a room. She had passed away years earlier, and that's where he stayed. We were both seventeen, and even though he was born a year before me, his birthday hadn't come yet. We talked some more, and it seemed okay at the time. I at least had a roof over my head and someone who cared about me.

I landed a job a few days later. I still didn't have a car, but he did. He didn't work, but he always seemed to have money. He drank beer, and I didn't like being around that. I finally met his family, and wow, I was surprised. There were many of the same dysfunctions, and even more that I had never experienced before.

His father died prior to me entering the picture, and his mother had a portrait of him over her bed in a casket. That was scary to me. The boy who later became my husband was the third-born child out of four and was eight years older from the youngest. He was a mommy's boy. Any time he wanted money for beer, she would hand it over or anything else he wanted. I was uncomfortable with this family, even though I liked his oldest and youngest brothers.

Months passed, and I still hadn't walked into a church to worship because I was angry. All I did was work and work. I finally knew I had to call my mom and dad; I missed and loved them no matter what. So just like Jonah, I had to let the fear go. I called them, and I visited the following weekend. There is no fear in love; perfect love expels fear. When I was afraid, it was because of fear of punishment.

So, life continued in New Hampshire for me and Massachusetts for my parents. We would talk on the phone, and I would visit them. My life in New Hampshire was mainly working and wondering what to do next. I was sad that I never graduated and began thinking I was with someone I thought I loved, but the problem was, he was an alcoholic. At seventeen, I had no clue what that meant. Through hard work, I was able to get an apartment. He still wasn't working, and yes, that upset me. His mother gave him money, so at least the basics were paid for between my job and that.

In the fall of 1975, I was sitting in a restaurant, and I got this bad feeling that something was wrong at home, so I called my parents. Sure enough, Grammy B, my dad's mom, had passed away less than thirty minutes before I called. We drove to Haverhill for Grammy's funeral; it was my first time at a wake and funeral, and there were feelings inside of me that I didn't understand. I kissed her forehead, and she was ice cold.

I now understand PTSD. Some of this came from her babysitting me as a child, and some from a birthday party for her when I was about five years old with most of the family there. This party started fine but ended in terror for me and, I guess, for some others as well. I cried the entire way home with my mom, my aunt, and her children in the car. I had nightmares because of this party— it created fear in me. Although I don't dive into the details, let's say it affected me forever.

By then, it was getting into the holiday season, and I was working two jobs and thinking of leaving my son's future father. I told him I couldn't take much more of the family's dysfunctions, so he threatened to jump off Suncock Bridge in New Hampshire if I didn't stay and marry him. I called the police, and he lied and told them he dropped his wallet. So, once I had my 18th birthday, we were married by a minister. His family and much of my family were there, but not my mom and dad. They refused to come.

The change was imminent. My new husband and I moved to Haverhill, Massachusetts, where my family was. We both got a factory job and had other couples as friends. Things were improving for a while. Daddy and I seemed to be working through the "big secret." My husband and I saw our friends with children, and we thought we needed to try and have our own family. I went to see my ob-gyn. He ran several tests and finally told me my right ovary didn't work. He gave me some pills hoping it might help with getting pregnant, and it actually worked! Thanks to God, Joshua was on his way.

I finally was able to buy my first car and didn't have to fear being a passenger and holding on for dear life. In 1972, I bought a lime-green Ford Pinto hatchback, and I was excited. I had purchased and paid for it myself, and it was mine. I had wheels, and I could go where I needed to. I had freedom. However, the family dysfunction continued on and off, and back then, there wasn't any place I could go because of my dad's "make your bed and lie in it" weighing on my mind. Because of this, my husband and I were separated on and off, and I always took him back.

It was time for Joshua to be born, and my husband was nowhere to be found. There was only my parents and my grandparents with me at the hospital. I let my Nana name my son Joshua, and I loved it! It meant strong and courageous and was from the Bible. Joshua was christened in my family church in December 1976. It was a wonderful day, and then the new year came around. My parents started going to church and becoming involved with the ministry. Every Sunday was a great church and family day, except my husband and sister never went.

Things seemed fine again for a while. I went back to work part-time, and he worked off and on. I came home from work one day, and he was in my bed with one of my friends, the woman next door. That was the last straw! Despite everything, I was nineteen and trying to make this marriage work. So, I told both of them to be gone by the time I returned.

We were separated once again, and Joshua and I were on our own... again. My husband kept calling, saying he would quit all his stuff, and pleaded for me to take him back. So, I finally took him back. That was a big mistake! It was the same old, same old. What I didn't know then that I know today was that others were telling him what to do. His mother had the apron strings, and so did his girlfriend. He hit me worse than ever this time and took off with my son. I tracked him down in New Hampshire, but because we weren't divorced, the police couldn't do anything. And then, there were two states involved. It was a mess.

He finally came back with Joshua, and once again, I tried to make the marriage work. Well, it didn't, no matter how hard I tried. We separated again, and I filed for a divorce. Neither one of us could seem to help each other, and we both had "baggage." You know, past stuff that towers over your relationship like a thundering cloud, waiting to tear loose at any moment. I couldn't let my son continue to deal with that, and I wasn't going to in my adult life, either.

The Bible says, "Therefore shall a man leave his father and his mother, and shall cleave unto his wife: and they shall be one flesh" (Genesis 2:24). Our vows say for better or worse, in sickness and health. The two good things from my marriage were my son's birth and my parents' forgiveness and healing for the "big secret." God's Word also says, "Having predestined us unto the adoption of children by Jesus Christ to himself, according to the good pleasure of his will" (Ephesians 1:5). This verse gives me comfort to know that His good will for us is immeasurable and that He planned for the Godly adoption of all of us unto Him. Romans 8:28-30 also says, "And we know that all things work together for good to them that love God, to them who are called according to His purpose." Even if we falter from the plan, God knows that we love Him, and He picks us up and continues on.

I was working, and Joshua was in daycare. Life was going well at this point. Yes, I still had questions about God, my life, but things looked okay. Joshua was growing and was healthy. I considered him a gift from God. In 1978, I got paid every two weeks, and my parents were paid weekly. I asked Daddy if I could borrow ten dollars until I got paid. He agreed. What luck I had with that ten-dollar bill! It turns out it was a counterfeit bill. He had no reason to think the bank would give him a fake ten-dollar bill, and low and behold; I was arrested for it.

The bank never took accountability for it even though my dad told them what had happened, and I was given a year's probation, and then the file was to be sealed (expunged) and never brought up again. It was dismissed; the judge knew I was not guilty, and after all these years, Haverhill, Massachusetts, still hasn't sealed the record.

Since 1978, I've worked and had background checks, never hiding this fact from anyone, and I passed with flying colors every time. In 2006, Monster Man used this against me from my social security number.

I allowed Joshua's father to visit because he was my son's dad, and at that point, I still didn't know much about my father. The visits were to be in front of my parents. He still wasn't changing and didn't go for any help. I refused to allow his girlfriend to visit my son. I reasoned that domestic violence and alcoholism aren't from God; it's from the enemy, Satan. God defeated Satan, and he wants to destroy God's children and families, like in the beginning with Adam and Eve. God said to multiply, be fruitful, and then the serpent came into the picture. There was too much yucky stuff going on in my ex's household.

Well, life went on; Joshua was in daycare as I worked. I was going to church; all the usual stuff people would do in life. Joshua and I were happy. Back in high school, I had always thought of joining the Army. My grandpa and dad were in the Army during the wars, so I wanted to carry on the torch. I went to talk to our local recruiter. And I had quit trying to mend my marriage.

I was so excited to join the Army. In December 1979, I was stationed for training in Missouri at Fort Leonard Wood; everyone called it "Lost in the Woods." It was the dead of winter, and it was brisk. But I was free, and I thought I was on my way to a new life for Joshua and I. Sure, I missed my baby, my parents, and everyone, but at age 21, I saw things I had never seen before. It was an exciting time, but some of it was frightening. I had questions about the way people lived and conducted themselves. There were former prostitutes, which I had no clue what that was. There were bisexuals. I didn't know what this was, either. There were also sexual harassment claims against authority figures, the drill sergeant mostly. I was shocked! They were living in my barracks and I didn't know what to think or how to act. I guess I was too young and had never experienced anything like that. I think my life was sheltered until that point. I made many new friends in the Army, and the way I looked at it, whatever they do is their business, not mine. I kept my head down and just followed orders. I was doing great, and my son was with my parents during my training. Everything was looking up. I had planned to return to school with the help of the Army and hold onto a promising career. I was excited and had hope.

Joshua in Ida's Army jacket and a general's hat.

My divorce became final in February 1980, and I was relieved, but it caused a problem; the recruiter had lied to my parents and me. The Army drill sergeant said no single moms were allowed. I tried to fight this action, but instead, my time in the Army was voided from records, even though I was there. I returned home to Haverhill,

Massachusetts, picked up Joshua, and returned to Missouri, hoping to change what had happened. There was a slew of injustice, and the recruiter misguided me and my parents by telling us if I gave my parents temporary custody, I could join the Army.

Once again, the predator, Marty, dug up my records from 1979 and twisted more lies about me. In 2006, he posted my military picture on eBay and sold it with the word MURDERER above it. And again, he got away with this.

Joshua and I went back to Haverhill, Massachusetts, and even though I was divorced, I tried one last time to have his biological father do the right thing. He was ordered to pay child support of 15 dollars a week and provide health insurance, but that never happened. I had full custody, and he still didn't change. One day, he asked to take Joshua to see his mother and never returned him. I went to court and filed papers against him, and he and his mother went to another court and lied. That court somehow granted him full custody of Joshua. I couldn't understand how the courts did this and so I began fighting for Joshua. I couldn't let my child be with him and the unfit "stepmom," who was actually his girlfriend. She had lost her children, and she wasn't about to raise mine, nor was I going to let his father show his abusive nature to Joshua. My duty as his mother was to protect him, so I took him and fled to a friend's house in Cheyenne, Wyoming.

I got a job, and Joshua was going to daycare. As I tried to sort everything out, my ex-mother-in-law tracked us down with her money. Somehow, the courts still were not working things out, so I was arrested and had a choice to make. I could fight the case in Wyoming or return it to Haverhill, Massachusetts, where I initially had custody. I chose to go home, and my parents were given temporary custody until the mess was fixed.

The case was dismissed on October 9, 1981, despite the injustice. I resumed full custody and continued to raise, Joshua. His father never complained about court orders.

Joshua Joking Around with his Grandfather

Ida, Joshua, & his Grandfather

4

What Is Grief?

"Jesus wept."

John 11:35

The Bible simply mentions grief as, "Jesus wept." Weeping is a feeling much more intense than crying or even sadness. It is a deep longing for someone or something that is beyond our control. When Jesus wept, he was experiencing a collaboration of sorrow from the people around him. He was feeling their grief and emotional pain.

Growing up, no one had ever told me about death or grief. I was told that different people, family, and friends passed away and were not coming back. It just stopped there. The first funeral I ever attended was in 1975. "Grammy" was in an open casket, and it looked like she was sleeping. No one explained what this meant or what had been left out of the equation. I guess I thought Grammy would be sleeping forever. At the viewing, I kissed her on the forehead, and she was cold, like my dealings with her when I was a little girl. Part of me was glad she was gone, and part of me wasn't. I didn't know how to deal with this at the time.

In today's world, different types of groups discuss grief. Some of these involve school counselors and therapy grief counselors. The publishing world is full of books and other resources to help with various types of grief and understanding its stages. There are now opportunities for people to be supported during these processes. In this chapter, I explain the different kinds of grief and the parts and mechanisms that help my process.

How do we even know what normal is? I have been asking this question over and over for a long time. Normal grief is defined as a person's reactions to a loss that involves an individual's feelings, emotions, and psychological and cognitive responses. The truth is that "normal" is what is normal for you. Normal grief pertains to my reactions to losing my son and others who passed away close to me. In some of those losses, I knew I would see them someday in heaven, and my grieving process was much easier to cope with. The ability to say "goodbye" helped with grieving over specific people in my life. There was closure. When I became a Christian, death was not just defined as a grave, as I had been told as a child; it's an eternal resting place.

No one can tell you how to grieve, but I can help with some of these processes. So, here are a few scenarios of "normal" grief. Is it normal to cry, even weep, for extended periods? Yes, is the plain answer. Crying is a part of the process. Is it normal to holler, shout, or even scream if it is a frightening situation within the loss? Yes. Our bodies frequently don't know how to react to situations initially. Sometimes, you'll even find yourself in a state of shock, and numbness floats over you. The replay of scenarios will even move its way across your thoughts.

Finding soothing music, talking to someone (letting it out), reading, researching, creating your own discussion groups, and making a difference in the lives of others (see Chapter 11: Resources Related to the Story) are ways that I worked through some of these. Some days you're fine, and some days you're not, which is normal.

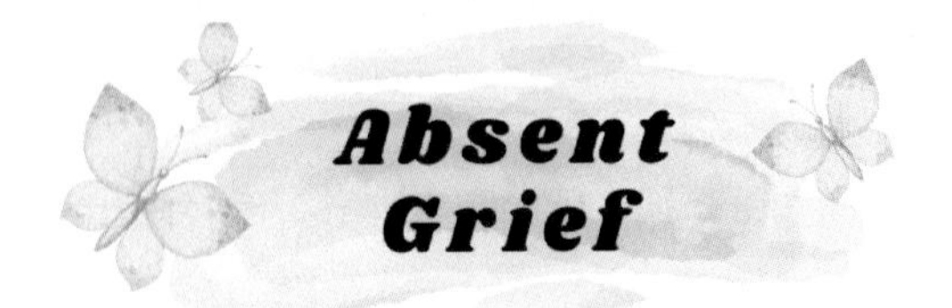

Absent Grief

We all experience absent grief when our loved one or friend dies. In my case, Joshua is now completely absent from my life. I was in shock and denial for a while. Coping with this as a mother, I screamed, kept saying no, and even called my son on the phone, but no one answered. In 2023, I know this was all part of normal and absent grief. It's only not normal if you stay in this cycle.

Collective Grief

Collective grief is a collaboration of grief created on a large scale. My first experience with this was the loss of a classmate named Robin. The teacher told the class Robin wasn't coming back because of a scuba accident over the summer, and that's all we were ever told. It affected me over the years, and I have thought about this often. Our teacher missed an opportunity to help all of us understand collective grief.

My second experience with collective grief was 911 in the September 11, 2001 attacks. Even though I wasn't there, it was tragic for the world; many of us grieved for all who were murdered. A majority of us can identify where we were when this occurred. My mom and I were watching Good Morning America; we had lost my dad a year earlier, in 2000. I couldn't believe what I saw but knew it was real. My mom was afraid to watch the clips. She said, "And you have always flown... that could have been you." As a mother, my first instinct was to call my son. Many of us reached out to our family members. This was part of us dealing with our collective grief.

I've thought about various stories of depression and how many people committed suicide or thought of it because of this particular grief. How many people were killed in the Holocaust? All the wars we have had in the world and all the mass shootings in different schools over the years have created collective grief. The one positive thing about collective grief is that we can comfort each other in some way, shape, or form.

Inhibited Grief

I have never experienced inhibited grief, but I know people who have. Some examples of this are leaving the bedroom the same as how their loved one who died had it last, drowning their sorrows in alcohol, or not dealing with the death and putting it to the wayside (just another day).

Abbreviated Grief

There were two people in my life with that I experienced this type of grief over, my best friend, Nancy, and my grandmother.

I knew Nancy was in heaven when she passed away. She died from cancer, but I couldn't be with her because of Monster Man. She and I shared many beautiful memories. We went on mission trips, participated in Relay for Life together, and celebrated Christmas and birthdays with each other. But the strong cord between us was the Lord. I will always love and miss her, but I will see her again one day.

Nana (my mom's mother) and I were always very close. She died from cancer quite suddenly. Before that, Nana called and thanked me for the flowers I sent because she had been sick. I didn't know she had cancer. Then, she told me that my uncle was taking everything out of the apartment and that she loved me. I couldn't shake my bad feelings, so I called my parents. Finally, my dad called me and told me that Nana was hospitalized. Thankfully, she knew Jesus, and I will see her again someday.

There was only a short time that I could grieve Nancy's death due to everything I was handling at the time. With Nana, there wasn't much time because she died so abruptly. Therefore, these instances are considered abbreviated grieving.

Masked Grief

I can also relate to this one in many situations. Masked grief is when someone tries to suppress their feelings or not deal with them at the time. This type of grief can be very harmful. It is the breach between staying in the past and moving forward. In other words, you are hiding behind a false premise. I feel as though masked grief tried to prevent me from doing many of the things I wanted to do. You have to learn to move on and push forward. Crawling into a hole and feeling sorry for yourself is not the answer, and not dealing with grief is also not the answer. You have to hit it head-on and accept that it happened. You could ask yourself, "Okay, what can I do now to better my circumstances or prevent someone else from going through the same thing?"

Secondary Grief

This is a big one for me! There is way too much revolving around secondary grief to even list all of it, and too many years that I went through secondary grief to put it all on paper. The sad part is I am still dealing with some of this. I couldn't protect my mom or my Joshua from all the tragedy. I tried with all my strength, but I couldn't control others' actions and choices even though my mother and son didn't deserve any of it.

When you lose someone special from your life, the things and people that follow that now are absent are considered part of secondary grief. These can be the change in atmosphere on a holiday because they are not there or a relationship that was held together because that person was alive. Secondary grief can be spurred on by a collection of memories or pictures found in a box. One of the crucial things I am dealing with is honoring my past loved ones properly.

Two of my family members do not even have their names engraved on their headstones. Before I pass on, I want them to be honored. Even the loss of my marriage, though I felt my divorce was right, brings secondary grief. Much of this grief can be overwhelming at times. My best way of passing this on is by enjoying the memories and thinking about new times ahead with those around me.

Disenfranchised Grief

Disenfranchised grief is the loss of a relationship outside the typical family structure. It can be the mourning of a far-removed or close friend or acquaintance. Sometimes, it is the unknowing of why a death occurred, such as the case of a suicide or overdose, that causes this type of grief.

My son had a very close friend who always called me mom since he was an adolescent. Years later, this young man committed suicide with a gun. I will never know why; his life looked okay, and he was even expecting his first child. But only God and he knew the reasons. Because of this death, Joshua and I took it hard. This is one part of my life where I experienced disenfranchised grief. Although he was close, he wasn't blood-related, and we felt sorrow for his family. The only other person who affected me this way was a young lady named *Sherry.

When Joshua was killed, all of his friends who had called me mom over the years and even the ones who knew me only as Joshua's mom were like family, not blood family, but as part of a special bond. Sherry was the only one who was sincere through Josh's tragic death and continued calling me Mama. She had problems, and I was trying to help her. But Sherry ended up going to jail and serving time. She called me, wrote me, and we made plans for her to come here after she got out of jail. The problem was Sherry didn't make a good choice the night she was released. I was told that she returned to drugs and died from an overdose. In the future, I would like to do something special in memory of her. I have known many people over the years who have had family members who committed suicide. Joshua saw many of his friends die and experienced disenfranchised grief on a large scale over the years.

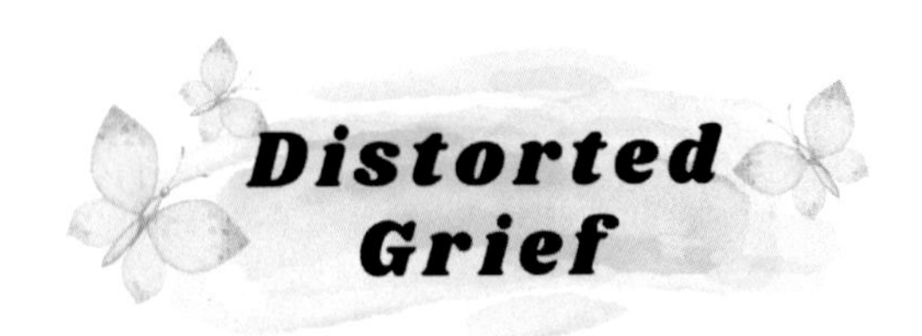

Distorted Grief

Distorted grief can be created from traumatic grief, which is the next section. When you feel people are not listening to you over the things that have happened, feelings can be distorted. They are not going to feel the same way as you do, or they may do strange things after someone's death that you may never understand.

Traumatic Grief

My sister, for example, took all of our family pictures and cut out my mom. She kept only pictures of herself and her dad in the frames. She even demanded to have their wedding rings.

I've experienced traumatic grief many times in my life. I actually have another son named Derek, who died at birth. I won't dive into the details of Derek's death because, honestly, it's not a picture that I would want in anyone's mind. To say it was traumatic is an understatement— this type of trauma sticks with a mother her whole life. Then, of course, the trauma of Joshua's death many years later added to this grief. I almost died from sadness.

As a mother, it was devastating in both cases. There was shock, disbelief, numbness, and so much more. Once the shock wore off, then depression and anxiety hit me. Then, the "what if," "could of," and "should of," questions flowed through my thoughts. With traumatic grief, I know the worst for me was making or not making impulsive decisions.

Cumulative Grief

This is the type of grief that builds upon itself. I look back and know that the tragic circumstances in my life were stacking and festering. Without the help of God, counseling, and therapy, I may never have been able to grieve in the usual way.

Exaggerated Grief

Nightmares, fear, and PTSD can all be signs of exaggerated grief. After the death of Derek, I had nightmares for a long time. What I know now is that I suffered from a type of PTSD. Some people may experience anxiety and depression because of this grief.

Anticipatory Grief

I have experienced this grief many times over the years. When you know a loved one will pass away, and you are unwantingly waiting for that phone call or the season they will go, we call this anticipatory grief. Only God knows when death occurs and within what season. So, we try and prepare ourselves emotionally, and we grieve even when someone is still alive.

Not seeing my granddaughters is very much like this to me. Even though they are alive, I grieve for them and have for years, and I pray for them always. I know Joshua grieved for them, too. For them not to be in our lives has broken both his heart and mine. You can never get memories or time back if they have been taken away.

Complicated Grief

This grief is a like being in a continuous, heightened state of mourning. It often prevents you from healing. In my opinion, it is a combination of grieving that causes this. You may have an ill parent close to dying, so you feel anticipated grief, all while your aunt has just passed away, and you can barely grieve over her because of you helping your parent, which creates delayed grief. This is a building of things and creates a complicated feeling. You may ask, "Why is all this happening?" You're not even sure how to take it all in. Then, your parent passes on, and you experience absent grief. It sounds complicated, doesn't it? Well, it is. All the factors you are going through at one time can lead to complicated grief.

Delayed Grief

Yes, I have experienced delayed grief. The tragic death of my son, Joshua, brought back all the emotional suffering from Derek's death in 1985. I think if I had dealt with Derek's old trauma at that time, there's a possibility I wouldn't have felt this delayed grief so intensely.

Chronic Grief

Chronic grief is very similar to complicated grief. With this, you often have difficulty resuming your everyday life, activities, and existence. Holding a job, attending school, or continuing a relationship may be challenging. It can be a destroyer, if you let it.

Conclusion

No matter who we are in this world, we all feel grief at some point. The death of my sons, Derek and Joshua, has been the worst type of grief I could've ever imagined. Think about your life and use the examples above to identify where you are in those spectrums with life-changing events. I have put chapters 6-8 in the book to show you how I've dealt with my grieving process. Hopefully, you find that they help you, too.

"The Spirit of the Lord God is upon me; because the Lord hath anointed me to preach good tidings unto the meek; he hath sent me to bind up the brokenhearted, to proclaim liberty to the captives, and the opening of the prison to them that are bound; To proclaim the acceptable year of the Lord, and the day of vengeance of our God; to comfort all that mourn; To appoint unto them that mourn in Zion, to give unto them beauty for ashes, the oil of joy for mourning, the garment of praise for the spirit of heaviness; that they might be called trees of righteousness, the planting of the Lord, that he might be glorified."

Isaiah 61:1-3

5

Who Was Joshua Kreiser?

Joshua Michael Kreiser

November 9, 1976 - December 30, 2020

Joshua had a beautiful and loving nature.
He cared about people and tried his best to do more for others than he did for himself. He was compassionate and was a positive leader to those around him.

Joshua's Life

Joshua was a gift from God and was born on November 9, 1976, at the Hale Hospital. You see, he was a miracle baby, as it was difficult for me to get pregnant. The doctors said I only had one working ovary. Uniquely, he was the only boy born in the hospital that day, and all the nurses went crazy over him.

Not wanting to deprive him on his first Thanksgiving, my mom and I put turkey, mashed potatoes, and all the trimmings into the blender, and Joshua loved it. Even though he ate baby food and Enfamil most of the time, Thanksgiving was a special time for our family. Unfortunately, I wasn't very good at taking pictures during that period and wish now that I had. *Putting food in the blender with milk or water is cheaper than baby food. It may sound a little unorthodox, but it's a helpful tidbit for new moms.*

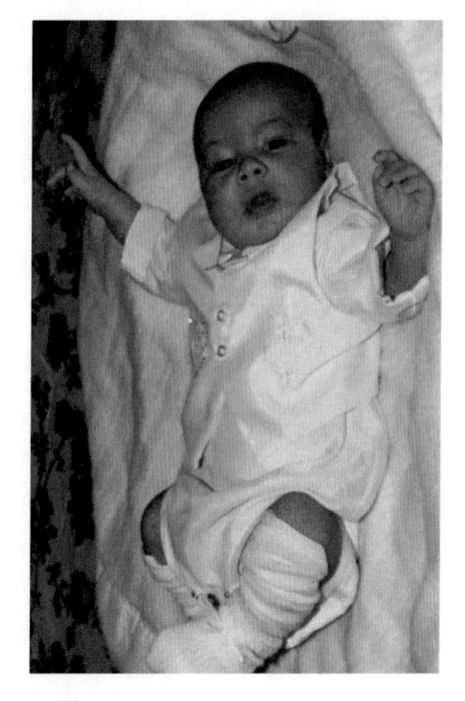

Joshua was christened in December of 1976 at Grace United Methodist Church. The day of the christening, my mom, God bless her soul, had apparently forgotten for a moment that Josh was a boy, and she'd not changed a diaper since I was a baby. When she attempted my son's diaper change, my mom got squirted! It was amusing at the time but also embarrassing for her. I get a chuckle thinking about it even 45 years later. My son also laughed when he was told the story. I miss the laughs from him.

Joshua was named by me and my Nana, Charlotte, after Joshua in the Bible, who had succeeded Moses and led the tribes of Israel into the promised land. I was married when I had Joshua, but his biological father and I were divorced due to domestic violence. The difficulties of being a single mom receiving no child support were insurmountable, but I ensured that Joshua was always well cared for. He attended school and church and was involved in community activities. He joined Tiger Cubs, Cub Scouts, and Boy Scouts. I had told him some of the things I learned while scouting over the years, and Joshua wanted to try it, too. I was a scout mom when he was growing up.

We also were involved at Twin Hills Park. Joshua played T-ball and football there, and as moms do, I worked in the concession stand. Like the other moms, we all took turns and would bring snacks for the teams our children played on. On the Fourth of July, we would watch the fireworks at Twin Hills Park, and we had many great times swinging and playing on the playground. In 1985 and 1997, we spent time with my parents when they visited. My last memory of the park was in 1997. My dad and Joshua were happily swinging and going down the slide.

I taught Joshua how to roller skate as a child, partly because I enjoyed it growing up. As a family, we participated in skate-a-thons at Hot Wheels in Crestview, Florida, to raise money and awareness for cancer. Many years later, I even took my granddaughter roller skating to try and teach her.

Later in life, Joshua kept the tradition alive of helping fundraise for cancer awareness, but this time he used his gift of singing and music to accomplish this. I went to all his shows over the years except the ones out of state. My duty as a mother was to support my son in his endeavors. Did I like the music? To tell you the truth, no. It was too loud, I couldn't understand many words, and the mosh pits scared me. Nevertheless, it was important to be there.

Joshua grew up attending church and attended church camp at Blue Lake Camp and Camp Wanakee, which he enjoyed. I also grew up going to Camp Wanakee.

Talking to God

I remember one weekend that Joshua had a friend stay over. I was on a prayer line praying for my marriage after we lost Derek. Joshua told his friend I was talking to God. His friend said, "I want to talk to God," so he did. It sounds pretty simple, and it was. Talking to God does not require much of a person. All he had to do was start talking like he was speaking to a friend.

Christmas Over the Years

Christmas was a special day in our lives. Joshua's first Christmas was spent with Nana and Grandpa (his great-grandparents). We always did Christmas Eve at their house for years, and that year was no different. Incidentally, Joshua was the only boy that was a great-grandchild. He and my dad (his grandfather) were very close and did fun "guy things" together.

There were some funny Christmas seasons, and I made some mistakes as a mom trying to protect my son from disappointment. When Joshua's biological father didn't do what he should have (and I was a single mom), I would buy extra things and label them "From Santa" or from his father and grandmother. I did this until Joshua decided to be adopted and on through most birthdays and other holidays. At that time, I thought I was doing the right thing. As my son grew older, I told him the truth, and he was understanding.

Joshua's daddy and I would put fake snow on the bottom of his military boots and make a track outside in the den where the Christmas tree was. I anticipated Christmas morning to see Joshua's excitement in his eyes and hear him shout, "Santa was here!"

Mother's Day Breakfast

One Mother's Day when Joshua was little, he made me a special breakfast in bed. He knew I liked coffee and grilled cheese. We'd always made grilled cheese sandwiches together on the stove. Joshua sure tried his best for that breakfast in bed. He poured a cold cup of coffee that his dad had left behind and made me a grilled cheese sandwich in the toaster, using two pieces of bread and two pieces of cheese he'd put into the slots. Needless to say, it made a mess, and that toaster ended up in the garbage can. Then, he went outside and picked a flower and put it in a glass to give to me. He definitely tried. It was a sweet gesture, and I was grateful. When he was younger, he would pick flowers in the yard and bring them to me. He always seemed to be considerate of me.

Star Wars Sleepover Birthday

We threw Joshua a big birthday party with his friends one year. After the birthday party, we had a big sleepover, including both boys and girls. The boys were in Josh's room, and the girls were in an extra bedroom. But, of course, I was awake all night long to make sure nothing was going on. It was the longest night of my life. They were talking through the walls. Every time one of them went to the bathroom, I was right there, literally watching these two bedrooms. That was the only coed sleepover he ever had because I would not do that again, and I don't suggest it!

Football

Joshua was playing football when Michael Jackson's song "Thriller" came out, and my son would do the moonwalk on the football field. It would grab the attention of everyone in the stands and his teammates. He just had that charisma about him. I had photos of this, but some of my pictures were destroyed because of the hurricanes.

Older Years for Joshua

Joshua never graduated from Crestview High School. The people he was hanging around with were not good influences, so he and I talked about it, and we agreed, no quitting school. We decided, however, that Josh could get his GED. He followed through and successfully received it.

When Joshua got his driver's license, I bought his first car. My parents didn't have the money when I was growing up, so I bought my own. Times were different when Joshua was growing up than in many ways back then. Joshua and his girlfriend were hanging around some people who were bad influences, and the next thing that happened... a wrecked car. Thank God no one was hurt, but I never bought him another car. Over the years, we still had a solid mother-son bond, but there were times when tough love and boundaries had to be established. I never stopped loving and supporting him even though I didn't agree with some of his choices.

A Few More Memories

Over the years, we made many school projects together; the planets and a volcano were fun ones. Joshua was amazed by something I did for many children over the years and at work for the military at Eglin Air Force Base with the 655 Unit. I would dress up in different costumes and have them specially made from a rabbit to rainbow bright and many more costumes.

Under-roo's Days

Do you remember Under-roos? I sure do; there were some funny and adorable moments. If you have yet to learn, Under-roos was a t-shirt and matching underwear with different comic book figures on them. I remember that Joshua often acted out some of these as a child. He would put on Batman and come racing to me from his bedroom. Joshua opened his arms and shouted, "data, data, data, data Batman." Then there was the Incredible Hulk, the green man. He wore this guy a lot, and Spiderman and many other characters were part of our lives, too. What happy days! I wish I could've kept those days forever.

First Time with a Policeman

Joshua and his friend were in the woods. Joshua was repeatedly told not to go in there because of the pond, snakes, etc. But this day, when they were in the woods, Joshua and his friend found stuff and brought it to the house. I was upset as a mother because he could have been hurt. First, they had a chest they dragged and wanted to keep it. The boys were mad because they found it and thought they could keep it. I called Crestview Police about it, and the officer came out. The officer was very friendly and explained to the boys a few things... 1. It wasn't safe to be in those woods, 2. Why the chest wasn't for them, and 3. What the laws were about that. Joshua and his friend, Luke, were in grammar school at the time, I wish I could remember the officer's name, but it was many years ago.

I have so many memories of my Joshua over the years; some were wonderful, and others, not so great.

More Background

Joshua was adopted in the 80s, which was his choice, and he changed his middle and last name. A few months later, I became pregnant, and as a family, we would listen to the baby's heartbeat through a stereo and a microphone. We were a U.S. Air Force family stationed at Eglin Air Force Base. During my pregnancy, I was flown to Keesler Air Force Base in Mississippi because of complications with the pregnancy. They were no help, and I spent approximately a week there. Then, I got flown back to Eglin in Florida. The day I ended up back at Eglin, I still had a nightgown on, and I sat in the lobby for hours, and no one would see us. So, my family and I went home without being seen. On August 22, 1985, I called Josh's babysitter because something was happening to my body. As soon as they drove out of my driveway, I was in the bathroom, and I had lost my son, Derek.

When the ambulance arrived, they brought me to Eglin; they had to do a blood transfusion because I had almost died. I kept asking about my baby, Derek, and no one would give me any answers.

During that time, Hurricane Elena showed up. A few days later, they discharged me, and because of Hurricane Elena, they refused to give me Derek's body. Come to find out, they conducted an autopsy without my or my husband's permission. In September 1985, they gave us his body separated into two Ziploc bags in a Styrofoam cooler. They refused to provide us with a birth certificate, death certificate, and autopsy report. We tried to have an attorney intervene and get answers, but Eglin refused to comply.

I didn't know how to explain everything to Joshua because I was grieving and having nightmares from the trauma. Eventually, I also lost my marriage. My son is buried in Hershey, Pennsylvania, with my ex-husband's father's grandparents. He does not have his name on the marker, and I hope he will one day. His name is Derek Kreiser.

Amidst all this, Hurricane Elena caused the roof to cave in over the den and the extra bedroom. Repairs had to be done. So, losing a child, having a hurricane destroy part of our home, and trying to explain the grieving process to my young child, Joshua, was difficult for us.

As a 64-year-old senior, I have lost two children due to tragedy under different circumstances. I was never allowed to say goodbye or see them as normal situations would allow. We had a happy family up until these times.

Ida & Joshua

Joshua & His Band

Ida's Father, Raymond

6
Letters & Prayers

To Joshua,

On December 30, 2020, you sent me wonderful beach pictures, and we were going to see each other on my birthday; we had a memorable time planned. That night, I received a call from the Highway Patrol, and they came to visit me. They said you were killed on Highway 98 in Okaloosa County, Florida.

I was very numb and devastated by losing you, my Joshua. Over the next few days, your friends would say words like, "I am sorry," or "He was wonderful... is there anything we can do for you?" Most of your friends called me Mom over the years, and we spent birthdays and Christmas doing cookouts, watching Alabama football, going to concerts, and even funerals together.

My days that were once filled with joy are now replaced with grief and despair. You are gone. You and I will never talk on the phone again... no more hugs, no more kisses. No more of anything.

Now, on my birthday, when you and I would've spent the day together, I am instead putting flowers and a sign on Highway 98. I can barely stand or breathe. You are gone; I laid where you were hit for a long time and sang to you and cried.

You were sent to the Pensacola Morgue, and because of Covid and other problems, I wasn't allowed to see you. It took a long time before you were transferred to the funeral home. I was a major wreck trying to do all this alone. The funeral home put out the death notice, and here I was, just trying to cope while the drama was flying in every direction from your friends and exes.

Joshua, I thought through the years about everything we did with your friend *Jerry. I thought that he really cared, but when push came to shove, I found out the truth. This was so sad and very disappointing to me. He would always call me Mom. Remember when you and your band ran out of gas in the middle of the night? I got up and drove to you to get gas so you and your crew could make it home. I surely remember. I reminded Jerry of that and other things the day at the funeral home. Would you even believe the girl he hitched a ride with was trying to take my funeral rights from me as your mother? You are my son. You will always be my son. I gave birth to you; no one will be allowed to do that. Well, that night, Jerry and I talked through the evening. He admitted to sabotaging you with some things that were not pleasant on one of the same weekends you came to see me. If you remember, I ended up in the hospital and I still have your letter you gave me. I forgave Jerry because that's in the past, but I wish he never did that to you. What was planned as a wonderful weekend turned into a nightmare?

I know we got past all that, and I am very proud of you for your better choices. You had quit the band and were getting away from many bad friends and their influences.

I am still angry for all the chaos (something I'm working through) and the person/s who killed you and your so-called friends and band members. There was no need for all the disrespect they caused and the mockery they made of your death. I am so sorry,

Joshua, that I could not give you the proper and peaceful funeral you deserved. You did have a nice funeral, but mostly with my friends only. I forgave *Carol for all she did over the years. I invited her to the funeral, and I was glad she came.

Your memorial box was beautiful— specially made with Alabama and Bruins symbols, a microphone, and your name.

I will always love and miss you, my Joshua, and I will continue fighting for justice for you.

Love you.
XOXO,
Mama

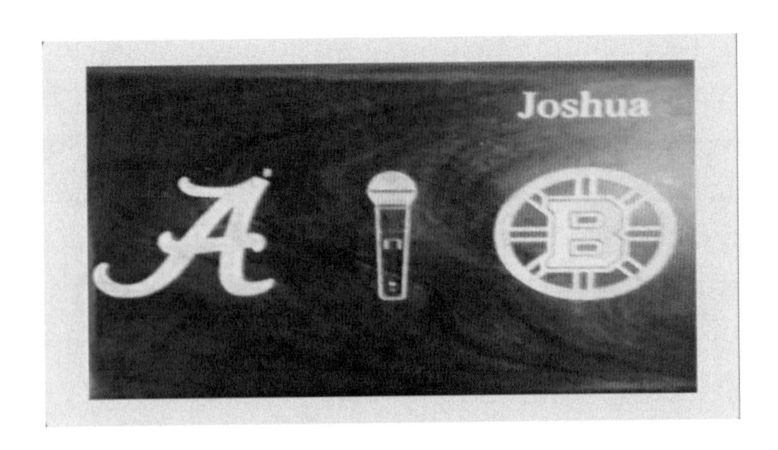

"ROLL TIDE"

Joshua loved
the University of Alabama,
the Boston Bruins,
and most of all,
singing with his band.
This wooden plaque was made after Joshua passed

*Dear *Sarah,*

To my precious granddaughter, Sarah. I always called you Gamma's Girl. I love you and miss you for who you are and who I am when I'm with you.

I thanked God for the day I learned you were on your way into this world. So did your great-grandmother, Clara. She made a video and sang two songs to you. She gave you a special message. She was so proud. She hoped and prayed that she would live long enough to meet you, but she passed away in November, and you were born the following April. I hope to share that with you before I pass away. If not, your mom has a copy to give you.

I know every moment we spent together was worth more than all the gold in the world. I know we can't ever regain our time, and I'm missing so much time in your life now. Gamma's Girl, I miss you so much. I think about you daily and wonder where and what you're doing.

I have many memories from when you were a little girl that I will cherish. After your dad passed away, I sent you several boxes of things I saved and bought for you over the years. I sent you money for birthdays and Christmas time, and Easter cards. Did you ever receive them? I guess it's out of my hands. Not a day goes by that you haven't been in my heart and mind. I miss your hugs and kisses. I love and miss you and hope and pray that we can get together before I pass on.

I remember when you first started swimming in our pool. You reminded me of your daddy at that age. He used to be a good swimmer, too. I remember us playing peek-a-boo; you would often hide behind the couch, and I would find you. I remember us playing with bubbles and so many other things.

You are 18 years old, and I've missed out on so much. That, too, has been out of my hands. One-quarter of my heart broke the day you were taken away from me. I have prayed that you would be happy and have all your dreams come true. When your daddy died, I invited you, your mother, and your great-grandmother to his funeral. I was hoping and praying you would come, but you didn't. That's not your fault. I'm sure you didn't have a choice.

I used to sing in your ear, "Jesus Loves You" and "You Are My Sunshine." One of the unique things I used to do, if you remember, was musical balloons. Of course, they were bigger than you, and I hope you remember them.

I miss you and love you.
XOXO,
Gamma

*Dear *Aria,*

I have grieved over you, Aria, who I always called Grammy's girl. Even though you are alive, you are not in my life because of family issues. All I wanted was to spend time with you, and I was prevented.

I want you to know how very proud I am of you. I know you haven't always had a good life. I'm sorry I couldn't protect you like I wanted to do.

We had a lot of beautiful times and adventures before you were uprooted. I remember them all. I hope and pray you do, too. You loved to swim, and we spent hours in the pool. We made movies together and went to some awesome places. I have two favorite memories of you, even though there are many great ones. The Goldfish! Do you remember the goldfish? That night it was like my mom was sitting right there with us; she loved her goldfish just like you. I also remember the time when I was teaching you how to spell daddy and grandma. That was a fun time, and I was so proud of you.

When we were in Connecticut, I was able to get you back in school for a short time and even sent you and your classmates Christmas presents. Then, you were uprooted again. Remember the time when I saw you and your half-sister at the movies? That hurt me pretty bad what you said to me. I know you didn't mean it, and I would imagine that someone had influenced you in that thought process.

I didn't see you again until my birthday when your daddy was killed. You wouldn't speak to me, and you wouldn't let me hug you. You were like a stone to me. You looked like Grammy's girl, a bit taller, but you didn't act like Grammy's girl. You were totally different. I felt the change in you. No matter your feelings toward me, I love you and always will. I shortened this letter for the book, but there is so much I want to tell you.

I love you and miss you.
XOXO,
Grammy

Prayers

Joshua never married but had two daughters.

Prayers for My Granddaughters

Dear Heavenly Father,

I pray that each will grow to have Psalmist's hearts and become virtuous women, as in Proverbs 31.

I pray they fear you because you are the Alpha and the Omega. You are the inception and the day we take our last breath; you are the only one who will never leave or forsake us.

Lord, I lift my precious granddaughters to you and ask for a hedge of protection around them. Please help them walk in your ways and obey your will. Hide them from any evil that may come against them. I pray specifically against all abuse. I pray that they take refuge in the shadow of your wings. I hope they feel loved and accepted as they grow older. Deliver their minds from any lies the enemy may have planted or try to use as deception in the future. Cause them to hear your loving kindness, grace, and mercy. Lord, let them grow in confidence and faith.

Manifest your love for my granddaughters daily, so they will see how awesome you are. May you give them a full understanding and complete knowledge of you and your love for them.

Bless them in their gifts and talents, and hide your Word in their hearts. Please watch over their minds, souls, and spirits.

I pray for two Godly husbands in their lives and that they raise their children by Godly statutes and commandments.

I pray they know you, God, and me as their grandparent and love us both.

Thank you, God, and I know your Word does not return void; your Word says that death and life are the power of the tongue, so I am talking life to my granddaughters and blessings over them.

I love and miss both of you and pray this over you in Jesus' name. **Amen.**

7

Friendship

"Greater love hath no man than this, that a man lay down his life for his friends."

John 15:13

What is Friendship?

True friendship can be a blessing. Life can be enjoyable, even in difficult times, when you know your friends are by your side. No matter what happens in your life, you can count on their encouragement, prayers, a person you can talk to, and someone who will listen to you and visa-versa. You can grieve with each other and support each other in every way. Sometimes our friendships are tested and tried, but if God is the central part, we can make it through.

Examples of Biblical Friendship

1. David and Jonathan— David and Jonathon loved each other. Jonathan even stood up to his father, King Saul.

2. Ruth and Naomi— Ruth would not leave her, no matter how tough things were.

3. Timothy and Paul were true friends— Paul was a great Christian mentor to Timothy. He chose him as his traveling partner on their disciple ship journey.

4. Jesus and the disciples— Jesus befriended Peter, Luke, Matthew, and the other disciples.

5. Shadrach, Meshach, and Abednego— Three young men who stood with Daniel against King Nebuchadnezzar.

There are many other examples of friendship throughout the Bible, but these are just a few examples that stand out to me.

My Friendships

Most of my closest friends either passed away or left me after the Marty fiasco, along with what Joshua's ex did to me on Facebook. However, my best friend, Nancy, stood by me. I miss her every day. We would talk about Jesus and what God's Word said. She also wrote letters to try and get me a safe place to sleep. I would pray for her and hold her bucket after her chemo sessions. We went on mission trips and Relay for Life fundraisers together. She was my Sunday School teacher, but she, unfortunately, passed away from cancer.

I want to make mention of a few of my other friends over time. I hope to have been as good a person to them as they have been to me: Paula, Peaches, Shirley, Colleen, a couple of my high school friends, and two friends from my grief group. I also have many long-distance friendships that I love, like sisters who have stood by me through thick and thin.

Without the people I have mentioned, I would have been a mess. I am also very grateful for newfound friendships, as God has allowed.

"It is better to trust in the Lord than to put confidence in man."
Psalms 118:8

8

Forgiveness & Unforgiveness

"And when ye stand praying, forgive, if ye have ought against any: that your Father also which is in heaven may forgive you your trespasses."

Mark 11:25

It took me years to be accepting of myself. Forgiving myself and others in my life was not an easy process. I had to go through some severe grieving to come to the place of forgiveness. I felt much shame and guilt over my circumstances through those bumps in the road and the people who aimed to hurt me.

Shame and Guilt

Shame and guilt are powerful words. Until you understand the meaning of those words, your life can be a rollercoaster, blaming yourself for various things. Despite everything, I tried to mold my life into how it needed to be. Did it all pan out the way I would have liked it to? No, it didn't. I had a myriad of people I needed to forgive, and I had to let go of all the shame and guilt. These are two little seeds that grow and prevent you from reaching forgiveness. Could I forgive them before they passed away, as my mom would say, "Going to H.E. double hockey sticks?" But she would also say, "Two wrongs don't make a right." She was right about the second one; I had to let go.

I had never heard the word "grief" until the 1980s. Grief is so much more than just a word. It's our emotions and feelings from our heart, soul, and mind collectively. You have to dive into them to understand forgiveness. I highlighted the types of grieving in Chapter 4, but to come to the place of forgiveness is the ultimate resolution.

Before Forgiveness:

- A feeling that you are doing something wrong.
- A feeling of abandonment when someone dies and never says they are sorry for what they did to you.
- You question God and heaven.
- A feeling of devastation and not relief.
- You remember the sorrow and pain of others and wonder if God punishes them.
- You wonder if those who hurt you are in heaven or hell.
- A feeling of sorrow for yourself.

During and After Forgiveness:

- Remembering people with happiness in your heart and knowing you will see them again one day.
- Allowing God to heal your heart toward others.
- Putting your worries at the foot of the cross and letting go of guilt, shame, and those who were determined to hurt you.
- Having compassion for others' circumstances.
- Prayer, prayer, and more prayer!
- Leading others to the Lord that you have had a conflict with.
- Helping others' relationships mend.
- Finding love in your heart toward others.

Love

"And now abideth faith, hope, love, these three;
but the greatest of these is love."
1 Corinthians 13:13

Love is only a short word, but it's more powerful than some people realize. Love involves affection, compassion, care, and self-sacrifice. To forgive, you have to love. In this chapter, I define the various types of love. As you read these, see what kinds of loving relationships you have.

1. Agape love from the Bible means the fatherly love of God for humans, as well as the human reciprocal love for God.
   "For God so loved the world, that he gave his only begotten Son, that whosoever believeth in him should not perish, but have everlasting life" (John 3:16).
2. Eros love is the physical, sensual intimacy between a husband and wife.
3. Philia love is affectionate love without romantic attraction and occurs between friends or family members. It happens when both people share the same values and respect each other.
4. Storge is love of bonds and shared experiences. This includes the love of a mother for her child, or the love between siblings.
5. Unconditional love, simply put, is love without strings attached. This is the love that we receive from Jesus. He wants nothing in return except for our love back.

"Jesus answered and said unto him, If a man love me, he will keep my words:
and my Father will love him, and we will come unto him,
and make our abode with him."

John 14:23

Examples of My Process of Forgiveness:

I have forgiven most people who have intended to hurt me or my loved ones over the years. There are still a few people I am working on forgiving. The following things helped me deal with this forgiveness over time. Forgiving helps us, but not forgiving hurts us. It can be a heart wrenching process and pulls at every fiber of your being. Visiting places and people was an essential aspect of my process of forgiveness. I went to many gravesites and homes of the people I needed to reconcile with.

I also wrote and sent many letters expressing our conflict, sometimes asking for their forgiveness or visa-versa. In other instances, forgiveness was for a later date.

One example of this forgiveness began at my grandfather's funeral. There was a strange woman whom I didn't know at the funeral. She and the others around her briefly spoke. The woman came and then left. I never understood who she was. At Nana's funeral, this woman showed up again. This time she sat with my mom, aunts, and uncle, and again there were intermittent exchanges. Years later, I discovered she was one of my mom's sisters, whom I came to know in July of 2000.

When my mom was dealing with cancer, I looked up my aunt, and she came to the hospital to see my mother. My mom and aunt had blamed each other for things they had nothing to do with. This had gone on for over 55 years. Basically, they had missed out on their lives together. We spent the day together at the hospital, and they forgave one another. That day was a transformation of hearts, and we were able to take pictures together. I was so grateful to God that they mended their relationship before they both passed. I never knew this aunt until that day, but I loved her and grieved over her death when she was gone.

Family ties and connections are invaluable to me, so here is another example of deflating the balloon of conflict. This particular time was with my uncle. He wanted to meet his granddaughter; he and his daughter had not been talking and didn't have a relationship. So, I searched and found her. They ended up meeting and began rekindling their relationship.

Mean words can damage the soul. Words can hurt more than physical pain. Mom always said, "Sticks and stones may break your bones, but words will never hurt you." This is the one thing my mom told me I'm afraid I must disagree with. At some point, you even have to deal with the forgiveness of people who have said hurtful things to you. Sometimes, they don't even know they have affected you so much. It will help if you try to forgive these people who have hurt you with their words.

Many years ago, I shared some personal things with my mom. At that time, she was dying. She compassionately said, "Sweetheart, I should have known." Those little words were a massive relief for what I had dealt with for so long. It was a precious moment. Isn't it amazing how one sentence can give you a sense of completion? I didn't blame my mother for anything, but she needed to at least know my feelings.

We all live with scars from our childhood. My mom loved me wholeheartedly, and I know she is in heaven. If you don't know how to tackle the wave of addressing conflict and don't want to "rock the boat," you should confess these things before the Lord. Pray for courage and that those you are reaching out to will receive understanding and a softened heart over the issues at hand.

Ida's Mother, Clara,
and Joshua

Ida & Her Parents
Destin, FL

Ida & Her Mother
Relay for Life

9
Cowards & Thieves

"For we wrestle not against flesh and blood, but against principalities, against powers, against rulers of the darkness of this world, against spiritual wickedness in high places."

Ephesians 6:12

The cowards and thieves have tried to ruin my life. It was a difficult time, but God's Word will prevail over their evil, willful, and intentional acts.

Part 1

In my case, the cowardly seed was *Marty. Due to my social security number being on a will and his twisted and lying tactics and access to a lawyer's office, this man tried to assassinate my identity.

It took me years to rebuild who I was, and nothing was ever normal again. Can you imagine waking up one morning and everything is gone because of a stalker? Well, it can happen. They put your name on a website— first, middle, maiden, and married. All your personal information, pictures are stolen from your house, prayer journals from many years, and your life's documentation. Can you even fathom this?

The police wouldn't do anything because this monster seemed to have "people in his pocket." One of his weapons was intimidation with the internet, and that was just the beginning. He was a predator, a stalker, a thief, and so much more.

The internet can be wonderful, but it can also be a killer for many people. I am a victim of internet crimes, and anyone could be next. My predator used old newspapers and public records that we were told were shredded by officials. He extracted my social security number and medical information from a will. He paid or intimidated doctors to get my medical records. He also paid two people to lie about me, which caused my false arrest. So, then he used my mug shots as wallpaper photos on the internet. He frightened me by phone with what they call "spoofing," when your own phone number shows up. He threatened my family and me, including Mandy, my dog. She was the last gift I gave my mom, which I took care of when she passed away. I love and miss Mandy, but I had to give her to the vet for her safety to find her a new home.

He crossed so many legal lines. Many times, claiming to be a lawyer, he sent "official" faxes and made phone calls on behalf of other people, and he even destroyed things that didn't belong to him. If the people around me wouldn't comply with him, he threatened them. Many friends told him to "buzz off," but others believed him. Only God and He know what his ultimate intent was. He did an excellent job of destroying my life in the natural, but God held me together in the spiritual.

This man committed perjury in court issues and faxed the Okaloosa County Sheriff with more lies. Marty is a coward. I relate him to a man named Haman in the Bible in the Book of Esther. He is a coward for everything he has done; he is either obsessed or just pure evil. Marty and another predator, Ellen, stole pictures from my home and sold them on eBay, which eBay allowed. Thank God I had another copy to prove what they had done because eBay has never made it right.

This predator even stole copyrights from different places in my life. He hacked into my classmates.com. He coerced a Heritage Garden employee to lie, yes, lie, on paper about how my dear friend Mr. Russell died (who always called me the daughter he wished he had). Marty told everyone I kidnapped Mr. Russell (his father) from the Twin Cities Hospital and left him to die at home alone, which was also another lie. Mr. Russell was transported to my house by the hospital to begin with hospice; there was no way he could've died in his home by himself. His son and others who knew him, did nothing to help Mr. Russell. My mom and I were close to him; we may not have been blood, but we were family.

That is my take on the predator, Marty, who tried to take ownership of my life! He was controlling another person's life without their consent! It is a form of intimidation behind a keyboard and monitor. If it weren't for my faith, I would have committed suicide. Thankfully, God kept me alive, but I lost my house, my dog (Mandy), my job, volunteer work, church, friends, and other things.

I think the worst part was how it hurt Joshua. He stood by me, knowing it was all a big lie, but when the predator had me falsely arrested and plastered in the Playground Daily News, that made everything worse. I talked to my son on the phone, but I was fighting for our lives back with everyone.

There are laws in place, but the problem is that Okaloosa County won't enforce them and didn't back then, either. I asked myself, "Who does he own," or "Who's afraid of him?" These people are also cowards. During that time, I even contacted President Obama, and no response. I reached out to Florida Governor Ron Desantis and people within local and state agencies. When this first began, the Governor of Florida was Charlie Christ. He, too, has yet to answer back. These officials need to stand up and do their jobs or be gone. Not all states are the same. There needs to be national federal laws to protect all of us, no matter the crime.

Part 2

After Joshua was killed on December 30, 2020, the cyberstalking ramped up once again on Facebook. The same type of tactics, but now new people with different names. Are they in it for the money? You bet they are. It all goes back to my granddaughter's mother with her friends and my son's ex-girlfriends.

My son was a painter by trade and was the lead vocalist in many bands over the years. Many of his friends died of an overdose or suicide, and my son and I were there for those grieving each death. Joshua helped families with benefits and gave them personal money. Often, he created benefit concerts for families, including ones for cancer patients and friends who died from other causes. My son quit the band a few years ago, and when he passed away, none of his friends were there for him, except that they created a benefit concert and a GoFundMe meant for his funeral fund. Sounds benevolent, right? Wrong. The problem was that the money never made it where it needed to go as promised. The amount was well over $4,000.

His so-called "friends" and band members even went as far as to lie and get information from the funeral home about what was and what wasn't owed. They even ruined the obituary in the newspaper with falsehoods. They stuck their tentacles into every aspect of Joshua's death and ruined what could've been a beautiful thing— friends and family coming together for someone they loved.

I pray the authority figures do their jobs, but these things happened almost 30 months ago. Not only do I want justice for these crimes, but also for my son's death. I want these cowards and thieves brought to justice in the natural.

As far as the spiritual, God always has the last say and He is in control.

10

Final Thoughts

"Trust in the Lord with all thine heart; and lean not unto thine own understanding. In all thy ways acknowledge him, and he shall direct thy paths."

Proverbs 3:5-6

I can't do much more until the arrest is made on Joshua's hit-and-run case. It has been nearly 30 months since it occurred. I am waiting until Okaloosa County makes the arrest for Joshua's justice.

Please follow the links in my book under the Resources Related to the Story to help prevent someone else from experiencing these travesties. I wouldn't wish this on anyone. I hope and pray this book helps someone out there and that they find solace after their tragic circumstances.

My son wasn't perfect, none of us are, but this should never happen to a child and their family. I live to see the justice for my son. I also pray to be in contact with my granddaughters before I pass on.

The I WILLs:

- I will continue to strive for the days when everyone understands and cares about hit-and-runs or that they no longer exist.

- I will continue to push toward a better justice system with the dealings of stalking, bullying, and cyberbullying.

- I will continue to push toward a better justice system for hit-and-run laws and cases.

- I will continue to look for answers and stand my ground on what is right.

- I will continue to remember both of my sons and honor them properly.

- I will continue to forgive.

- I will continue to heal and lean on God for comfort.

11

Resources Related To The Story

"Be not overcome of evil, but overcome evil with good."

Romans 12:21

Arrival at truth requires vigilance, dedication, and perseverance. When something tragic happens to your family member or friend with unknown circumstances attached, you must arrive at truth by "getting the word out." Others will be willing to help and dive in. I am thankful to all the TV stations, newspaper journalists, artists, cameramen, organizations, and various committee members for their help. As a result, the following information includes links on how I was able to accomplish "getting the word out" and making a change. Some of these items may also help you cope with your own tragedies and make others aware of your dealings.

The websites, Facebook pages, letters, activism, and videos are a few things that I worked on post Joshua's death. I want to make a difference and show people that there are ways to help stop crime. If I can do it, so can you! Together we can make a difference. (For specific thanks, please see the Special Thanks pages.)

For E-Reader convenience, click on the hyperlinks below.
For Paperback reader convenience, scan the QR Code to my website page for all links or scan the QR Code for my Facebook page.

OR

Go to: www.pipstones.com/insearchofjustice

Webpage

Facebook Page

Okaloosa County Hit and Run:

VIDEO: State troopers investigate deadly hit-and-run in Okaloosa County - YouTube

Emerald Coast Crime Stoppers:

Emerald Coast Crime Stoppers July 2022 - YouTube

A Parent's Tragedy in Memory of My Joshua and Other Children:

Facebook Page Link

**Mayor James Fiorentini's The Haverville Gazette-
October As Pedestrian Safety Month:**

Article Page Link

Please Meet with Me Florida Governor, Ron Desantis: A Northwest Florida Mother's Plea:

YouTube Post Link

Escambia County Commissioners Meeting:

Meeting Link for Hit & Run Awareness Help – View at 12:25

Okaloosa County Mother Brings Awareness to Pedestrian Safety After Losing Son in Crash: Wear TV

https://weartv.com/news/local/okaloosa-county-mother-brings-awareness-to-pedestrian-safety-after-losing-son-in-crash#

Hit and Run Leaves One Dead in Okaloosa County:

WJHG Article Link

Pensacola Mother Looking for Justice after 2 Years:

WKRG Article

Graffiti Bridge: Graffiti Bridge Facebook Link

The Truth About Ida Kreiser:

Wordpress Blog

T.V. Videos:

Brent Kearney TV Facebook Link

Tanner TV Facebook Link

WEAR ABC 3 News, Pensacola

Facebook Videos Highlighting Joshua's tragedy:

Facebook Video 1

Facebook Video 2

Facebook Tree Dedication Pictures

YouTube Page:

YouTube Link Joshua Kreiser

Project Cold Case:

https://projectcoldcase.org/

Projects In Progress:

- Grafitti Bridge: 3 Separate Paintings
- Light-up Billboard: Hwy 98- Hit-and-Run Awareness In Memory of Joshua
- Hit-And-Run Awareness Month
- Hit-And-Run County-Signed Declarations for Designated Days
- On April 28, we planted a tree in Joshua's memory in Crestview, Florida.
- The DOT (Department of Transportation) is putting up crosswalks and lights and the State of Florida has agreed to pay for them.
- Crosswalks and Lights Link

Help For Crime And Grieving:

Project Cold Case:

https://projectcoldcase.org/

Mothers Against Drunk Driving:

https://madd.org/

Grief Groups:

Grief Group Link

Parents of Murdered Children Counseling:

Counseling Link

Asa Magoon Reference – Asa was a normal person, just like us:

A look back at the wrongful hanging of Asa Magoon

General Telegraph News; Hanged for a Brutal Murder. Asa Magoon, On The Scaffold, Protests His Innocence: *This link has since been taken down from the New York Times*

Graffiti Bridge Murals

Special Thanks

I would like to extend a special thanks to all the businesses and individuals who helped me overcome a variety of obstacles. Thank you to all those whose encouraging words, actions, and giving of their time, energy, and donations helped ignite the fire to accomplish the many things that we did together. I appreciate the businesses who allowed me to administer an event at their property site and others who created memorial certificates or other items in Joshua's name. You have all helped Joshua's death to not be in vain and for that, I am forever grateful.

List is in alphabetical order.
Please note that if an individual or business is not mentioned, it is not intentional.

Academy Sports & Outdoors, Pensacola, FL.
American Red Cross North Florida Region
Arby's, Pensacola, FL.
Ascension Sacred Heart Rehabilitation, Pensacola, FL.
Bounce House, Pensacola, FL.
Captian D's, Pensacola, FL.
Cheddars, Pensacola, FL.
Chuck E. Cheese, Pensacola, FL.
City of Haverville, Mayor James Fiorentini, Haverville, MA
City of Mary Esther
City of Mary Esther, Mayor Chris Stein
Cordova Bowling Alley, Pensacola, FL.
Corporal Whipple, Florida Highway Patrol
Dickey's Barbeque Pit, Pensacola, FL.
Dominoes, Pensacola, FL.
Drivingdownheartache.org
Eagle Tribune, Haverville, MA
Emerald Coast Crime Stoppers
Escambia County Sheriff's Office
Ferrovial, Street Sign Maker
Florida Department of Transportation
Florosa Fire Department
Former Mayor of Destin, Florida, Gary Jarvis
Former Mayor of Mary Esther, Florida, Margaret McLemore
Former Mayor of Pensacola, Florida, Grover Robinson IV
Gulf Power Company

Haverville High School Class of 1975 & 1976
Home Helpers Home Care of Pensacola
Ideal Optical, Pensacola, FL.
IHOP, Pensacola, FL.
John McMahon Environmental Center, memorial tree planted, Crestview, FL.
Lamar, Billboard Sign Creator
Mayor of Fort Walton Beach, Florida, Dick Rynearson
Mayor of Niceville, Florida, Daniel Henkel
Moe's Southwest Grill, Pensacola, FL.
Mypanhandle.com News
NHL Boston Bruins
Office of the Mayor, City of Crestview
Party City, Davis Hwy, Pensacola, FL.
Pho Real, Penscaola, FL.
PoFolks, Pensacola, FL.
Project Cold Case, Inc.
Restaurant Guru, Pensacola, FL.
Saltgrass Steakhouse, Pensacola, FL.
Santinos Pizza, Pensacola, FL.
Skyzone, Pensacola, FL.
Sonny's BBQ, Pensacola, FL.
Taylors Breakfast and Lunch, Pensacola, FL.
TBS , Fort Walton Beach, FL.
The Graffiti Bridge, Rodman & Joseph
Tyler Kercher, State Farm Insurance Agent, Pensacola, FL
University of Alabama Athletics Department
Unknown Name, Creator of Hit-And-Run Flag
Waffle House, Pensacola, FL
Waterfront Mission, Pensacola, FL.
Winn Dixie, Pensacola, FL.
WKRG News

Certifications, Appreciations & Recommendations

Red Cross HIV/AIDS Certification
Adult, Child, & Infant CPR
Introduction to Disaster
Home Health Aide
Nursing Assistant
First-Aid Basics
Certificate of Phlebotomy
Letter of Appreciation, Pre-K Teacher
Literacy Program Letter of Recommendation
Certificate of Appreciation, Meals on Wheels
Certificate of Appreciation, Guild for Divorce Recovery Workshop

Volunteerism

Relay for Life
Shelter House
Relay for Life
Baptist Health
Waterfront Mission
Bras Across Bridges
Skate-A-Thon Benefits
Salvation Army, Disaster Relief
Fundraisers for Families and Individual Needs

Schooling

Okaloosa Applied Tech
Pensacola Junior College
Northern Essex Community College

Author Biography

Some people are born to be an influence of compassion upon humanity. They are helpers, almost visionary. They see a need and fill it abundantly. They are well-equipped with diverse talents, inner strength, experiences, and enthusiasm. Being equipped is usually an outcome of lessons learned dealing with tragedy and standing in adversity. So, it has been with Ida's life of volunteerism and dedication to the community and others. Selfless love has been her motivation.

Ida Marie Britton entered the world in Cleveland, Ohio. The first transition in her life came on her third day. Ida and her mom, who was physically not well, were flown by helicopter to Haverhill, Massachusetts. What Ida didn't know was that she and her mother were fleeing a dangerously abusive situation that ended in divorce.

Ida's first year was spent with Grandpa, Nana, and Mommy. She flourished. Her mother healed, met, and married a man known to Ida as Daddy. Though they were hard workers, neither one had received an education beyond the sixth grade. Ida wanted to achieve more in life and prove herself.

The Grace United Methodist Church in Haverhill was the center of the only allowed extracurricular activities. She was a brownie and a girl scout, a member of the children's choir and, later, the adult choir. She loved her youth group and attended a youth camp in New Hampshire. At age eleven, Ida volunteered to babysit for a lady in the church. This little one was Down Syndrome. Ida was hooked. She would continue volunteering all through high school with special needs children. If there was a bake sale or a special dinner event, Ida volunteered.

In the 70s, she became a Candy Striper at Hale Hospital under the supervision of Mrs. Esther Roberts. Ida credits her with being a wonderful woman. This experience had driven a love for volunteerism deep into Ida within the medical arena. Simultaneously, her love of learning and insatiable desire for knowledge was in full bloom. This, however, was interrupted by a rather significant event.

While volunteering at the high school office, Ida read her personal file. She was adopted. As a result, Ida left home at age seventeen. She never graduated but later received her GED.

This "interlude" in Ida's life was not a season of volunteerism but gave her various skills and newfound independence. At age eighteen, Ida married a "mama's boy," and she was the adult in the relationship. Even though their marriage was rocky, she found intense joy in the birth of their first son, Joshua. Shortly after Joshua was born, Ida filed for divorce.

In 1979, Ida joined the Army, but because her divorce was finalized during boot camp, they terminated her enlistment. At that time, the Army didn't allow single mothers to be in the service. This was a temporary setback for Ida until she remarried and was pregnant with her second son.

With no emergency services available during Hurricane Elena, Derek died at birth. This was a traumatic time for Ida, but she continued to pick up the pieces and move forward. Later, the marriage began to disintegrate and ended in divorce.

Ida acquired a love of Florida, The Sunshine State. She again established a life of working and volunteering for a variety of organizations and with the elderly. Her son, Joshua, was involved in many of these activities.

The hit-and-run tragedy of Joshua at the young age of forty-four, led Ida to write this book. The warmth of Pensacola, Florida, is her home as she strives to arrive at the truth of her son's death. As a Christian woman (saved in 1987), Ida knows there is hope through Christ and prays that this book will touch the lives of many others who have suffered emotional trauma and have been victims of similar circumstances.

Made in the USA
Middletown, DE
14 October 2023